TABLE MANNERS WORKBOOK FOR KIDS 4-12

40 + Fun Activities to Teach Your Children Eating Habits and Behave in A Better Way in Front of Others

By

J. Hines

SHMAG PUBLISHERS

About the Author

J. Hines is a clinical psychologist and leading expert in the field of child and adolescent behavior. The author has written several books on the topic of child and adolescent behavior. These books offer a comprehensive and practical approach to addressing challenging behavior in children and teens, and provide parents, educators, and caregivers with the tools they need to effectively understand and manage difficult behaviors.

In his books, he emphasizes the importance of understanding the underlying causes of challenging behavior and working collaboratively with children and teens to find solutions. He also stresses the importance of empathy and understanding the perspective of the child and teaches the reader how to build a positive relationship with the child and how to help the child to develop problem-solving skills.

CONTENTS

Chapter 4: Fun Activities to Teach Good Behavior and Table Manners to Kids   43

Chapter 5: Dining Etiquette & Table Manners   51

INTRODUCTION

Table manners are crucial to daily living as they contribute to a pleasant and courteous dining environment. Teaching children proper table manners at an early age can aid in developing vital social skills that will benefit them throughout their lives. Children need to learn table manners because they help them become more thoughtful and courteous of others. When taught proper table manners, children learn how to share, take turns, and consider others' needs.

Children who have good table manners also do better in other social situations. Children who are taught proper table manners can feel more at ease and confident in social situations like family get-togethers and formal dinner parties. The ability to foster appropriate eating habits in youngsters is another vital benefit of table etiquette. Children are taught good eating techniques to learn to chew their food thoroughly, take little pieces, and eat slowly. Kids must avoid overeating and other harmful eating behaviors. Additionally, good table manners encourage wholesome conversation and enhance dinner enjoyment.

In conclusion, educating kids about proper table manners is essential to their overall growth. Children benefit from it by gaining valuable social skills, coming across favorably in social settings, forming healthy eating habits, and making meals more pleasurable for everyone.

The book includes interactive exercises and activities to help kids practice and reinforce the ideas they have learned about table manners. Each chapter also provides pieces of advice and ideas for parents and caregivers on teaching table etiquette at home. We

make the topics in the book simple for parents to help kids understand with the help of images and activities. We also offer real-life examples for parents to make their kids learn and use the manners in various contexts. We also go through more complex subjects like using a napkin, passing the plates, and setting the table properly.

Table Manners for Kids 4-12 is a thorough manual created to teach kids the fundamental principles of table manners playfully and engagingly. Children can learn how to act responsibly at the table and gain the confidence they need to share meals with others by adhering to the advice and rules in this book. It will therefore be a wonderful addition to any child's library and aid in their development as courteous people.

HELLO GROWN UPS!

Early age life skill training is important for kids because it helps them to develop important social skills such as table manners, communication, and teamwork. These are essential for children to learn at a young age as they will be useful throughout their lives. It helps to build self-confidence in kids. When children learn new skills and apply them successfully, it can help to boost their self-confidence and self-esteem. Life skills such as time management and organization can help children learn responsibility and become more independent.

It prepares them for the future by learning life skills at a young age; children will be better prepared for the future and more likely to succeed in school and their future careers. Table manners and other life skill training can help children become well-rounded individuals who can navigate various situations and interact with people from different backgrounds. Early-age training can help children develop critical thinking and problem-solving skills and improve overall wellbeing in children. Children who learn life skills at a young age tend to have better mental, physical and emotional well-being.

In addition, early-age life skill training, including table manners, is important for your kids because it helps children to develop important social skills, build self-confidence, teach them responsibility, prepare them for the future, help them to become well-rounded individuals, develop critical thinking and improve overall wellbeing.

You can help them easily learn table manners at a younger age. It will be simpler for kids to acquire and form good table manners as habits the earlier you begin educating them. Children learn best through repetition, so it's important to consistently reinforce the table manners you are teaching them.

Kids learn by observing and mimicking the adults around them, so it's imperative to model good table manners yourself. Kids have a short attention span, so it's important to keep the lessons simple and easy to understand. Use simple language, clear instructions, and repetition to help them remember the concepts. Visual aids such as illustrations, diagrams, and videos can help. Use these aids to help your kids understand the concepts more easily.

Kids are more likely to retain information actively engaged in the learning process. Incorporate interactive activities such as role-playing, matching games, and quizzes to make learning more engaging. The more opportunities children have to practice table manners, the more likely they will remember and use them.

Encourage children to practice table manners and give positive feedback when they do well. Avoid criticizing or scolding them when they make mistakes; give them constructive feedback and help them improve.

By incorporating these methods, it will be easier for kids to learn table manners at a younger age, and they will be more likely to adopt them as a habit. Use interactive activities, which are more likely to retain information when actively engaged in the learning process. Try incorporating interactive activities such as role-playing, matching games, and quizzes to make the learning process more engaging.

Give your kids examples of how to apply table manners in real-life situations. It will help them to better understand the concepts and see how they can apply them in their own lives. Incorporate humor, songs, and other forms of entertainment to keep children engaged and make the learning process more enjoyable.

Encourage the whole family to participate in learning table manners together. This can make it more fun and engaging for kids and help reinforce their learning concepts.

By incorporating these methods, learning table manners will be more interesting for kids, and they will be more likely to retain and apply what they've learned.

HI LITTLE ANGELS!

Yes, it's significant to learn good table manners to make a good impression on others. When you have good manners, it shows that you are respectful and considerate of others. Always be polite, use your utensils properly, and don't talk with your mouth full. These seemingly insignificant deeds have a significant impact on how others see you. And it will make you feel more confident and comfortable in social situations.

Dear kids! learning good behavior is crucial for you as it sets the foundation for your future interactions with others in society. Good behavior is not only important for making a good impression on others, but it also helps you to develop self-discipline, self-esteem, and self-control. When you behave well, you will compel other people to respect you. In addition, it is the key to successful personal and professional lives.

You must understand that good behavior includes being respectful, polite, and considerate of others, and also includes showing good table manners, being responsible, and being honest. It also includes being kind, empathetic and compassionate. It's important to know that your actions have consequences, and good behavior is about following rules and making the right choices for yourself and others.

Practicing good table manners and behavior can help you develop into a kind, respectful, and considerate individual. Good manners and behavior are important when eating at the table and in all aspects of life. They are the foundation of good communication, relationships, and social interactions.

It's also significant to remember that learning good manners and behavior is an ongoing process that takes time, practice and patience. It will help if you are mindful of your actions and words and always strive to be the best of yourselves.

It's also important to note that being a good human is not only about what you do but also about who you are. Being a good person is about being honest, responsible, and respectful. It's about being kind, compassionate and understanding. And also about being open-minded and curious. In short, good manners and behavior are about following rules and developing good character and being a good human.

CHAPTER 1 ALL ABOUT EATING HABITS AND TABLE MANNERS

Table manners are an important part of social etiquette and can make mealtime a pleasant experience for everyone. It's never too early to start teaching kids good table manners, as it can help them feel confident and comfortable in social situations. Teaching children good table manners is an important aspect of their upbringing that can have a positive impact on their social and personal development.

1.1 Eating Habits and Table Manners

Eating habits refer to the practices and customs associated with food consumption. These can vary greatly across different cultures and regions. Table manners are the rules we follow while eating, such as using utensils properly, not talking with food in one's mouth, and not reaching across the table. Good table manners are considered polite and help create a comfortable atmosphere during a meal.

1.2 Importance of Good Eating Habits

A healthy diet is essential for your child's growth, development, and well-being. When children eat well, they are less likely to grow up with chronic conditions, including heart disease, type 2 diabetes, obesity, and several malignancies. They will also feel better and have more fun as a result.

Children must engage in physical activity and eat the right foods to balance their energy needs and maintain a healthy weight.

These food groups should be included in a child's diet in a wide variety of foods:

- Veggies, fruits, pulses, and beans

- Lean protein, fish, poultry, or alternatives; wholegrain cereals are preferred. This comprises bread, rice, pasta, and noodles.

- Yoghurt, cheese, milk, or replacements

- Full-fat milk is recommended for children under 2; however, older kids and teenagers can drink reduced-fat variations.

- Children should avoid foods with added salt, sugar, or saturated fat.

- Help them to stay hydrated by taking enough water.

1.3 Eating Habits and Table Manners Are Inter Connected

Eating habits and table manners are interconnected. Table manners show respect for the food, the people around you, and the eating occasion. Eating habits refer to the way food is consumed considering its health benefits; table manners are the way food is consumed in a socially acceptable way. Good table manners can help create a comfortable atmosphere during a meal, while good eating habits can help ensure that people get the nutrients they need.

For example, good table manners dictate that one should not talk with food in their mouth and should use utensils properly, both of which can help improve the overall eating experience and make it more pleasant for those around the table. On the other hand, good eating habits such as eating slowly, savoring each bite, and not overeating can help with digestion and promote a healthy diet.

In summary, good eating habits and table manners go hand in hand to ensure that people eat in a way that is both healthy and respectful and promotes a positive social experience.

1.4 Teaching Kids Good Eating Habits and Table Manners

There are several ways to help teach kids good eating habits and table manners. Children often model their behavior after the adults around them, so parents and caregivers need to practice good eating habits and table manners themselves.

Eating together as a family can help establish regular mealtime habits and allow for the teaching and reinforcement of good table manners. Allow children to make their own food choices and serve themselves within reason. This can help them develop self-regulation skills and a healthy relationship with food.

Teach kids the value of a healthy diet and how various foods contribute to sustaining a healthy body. Make mealtime fun by encouraging children to try new foods or creating a themed meal or food challenge. Reward children when they demonstrate good eating habits and table manners; this can encourage them to continue practicing these behaviors.

Consistently reinforce good eating habits and table manners. When children make mistakes with their table manners or eating habits, correct them gently and explain why their behavior is not appropriate.

1.5 Teach Step-by-Step According to Kid's Age

Teaching table manners and good behaviors to children can vary depending on age. Here are some step-by-step suggestions for teaching table manners and good behaviors to children of different ages:

Preschoolers (3–5 years old):

- Start by introducing some basic manners such as keeping elbows off the table, not reaching across the table, and not talking loudly.

- Begin to teach them how to use utensils correctly.

- Teach them how to set the table and properly use serving utensils.

School-aged children (6-12 years old):

- Review and reinforce previously taught manners.

- Teach more advanced manners, such as properly using a knife and fork and holding a glass.

- Teach them how to properly clear their plate and utensils.

- Encourage them to participate in meal planning and preparation.

- Encourage them to try different foods and eat a balanced diet.

- Teach them the importance of being considerate to others while eating.

Teach table manners in real-life situations, such as during mealtime at home or while eating at a restaurant. It helps children learn how to apply their manners in different environments. Regularly reinforce the importance of table manners, and remind your child of the rules and expectations.

1.6 Stay Calm and Consistent

Staying calm and consistent is important when teaching your kids good behavior and table manners they should adopt in front of others. Communicate what you expect in terms of manners and behavior, and make sure that your expectations are age-appropriate.

Teaching good manners including table manners takes time and patience. Be consistent in your efforts, and keep going even if your child needs to pick up on the manners immediately. It can encourage them to continue using good manners example.

Avoid criticizing or punishing your child for bad table manners or bad behavior if something happens; gently guide and redirect them to the appropriate behavior.

Keep your emotions in check when teaching your child good manners. Children respond better when they feel safe, secure and not threatened. Use language your child can understand, which will help them understand the importance of manners and how they should behave.

By staying calm and consistent, parents and caregivers can help children develop good manners that will serve them well throughout their lives.

CHAPTER 2: IMPORTANT TABLE MANNERS FOR KIDS 4-12

Some important table manners for kids are as under.

- Don't slouch while sitting; keep your arms off the table.

- Utilize utensils correctly and refrain from messing with them.

- Only begin eating once every person has received a meal.

- Don't chat while you're chewing, and keep your Mouth shut.

- Cleanse your face and hands with a napkin.

- Thank the host or cook for dinner.

- Avoid leaning across the table for utensils or food.

- Before you get up from the table, ask to be excused.

- Refrain from playing with your food or making a mess.

- Clean up after yourself and assist with clearing the table if needed.

Now we will discuss some important table manners in detail. You must realize your kids to follow them strictly.

2.1 Wash Your Hands Before Meals

Washing your hands before meals is an important practice in maintaining good hygiene. It helps to remove any harmful germs or bacteria that may be present on your hands, which can then be transferred to food and potentially cause illness. A minimum of 20 seconds should be spent washing with soap and water, especially after using the washroom or handling raw meat. It will aid in reducing the spread of infection and disease.

Wash Your Hands		
1 RINSE	2 USE SOAP	3 SCRUB 20 SECONDS
4 RINSE		5 DRY

2.2 Keep the Napkin on Your Lap

"Keep the napkin on your lap" is a phrase commonly used while teaching table etiquette to remind people to place their napkin on their lap while eating. This practice is considered polite and helps to keep clothing clean during a meal.

Having a napkin on the lap during a meal is seen as a sign of good manners and shows respect for oneself and the company one is dining with. The napkin can be used to wipe one's mouth, clean hands, or to catch any spills or crumbs that may occur during the meal.

In formal dining settings, the napkin is typically placed on the lap as soon as one sits down at the table. In more casual settings, the napkin may be placed on the lap after food has been served. keeping the napkin on your lap is a simple and practical way to maintain good manners and cleanliness while dining.

Teaching kids to keep a napkin on their lap while eating is good. Not only is it good manners, but it can also help keep their clothing clean. It's also a good idea to teach kids to use the napkin to cover their mouth and nose when they cough or sneeze. This can help prevent the spread of germs.

2.3 Wait for Everyone

Teaching kids to wait for everyone at the table to be served before starting to eat is an important part of manners and social etiquette. It helps to foster a sense of community and mutual respect among those eating together. Additionally, it can also be a good time to take a moment to say grace or a prayer before starting the meal.

It also teaches patience, respect and table manners. It shows that they are aware of others and not just themselves. It can also be a good way to start conversation and bonding with family and friends.

Encouraging kids to be patient and waiting for everyone to be served can also help to prevent them from overeating or eating too quickly.

2.4 Do Not Pick Food

It is considered impolite to pick food with your fingers while eating. Instead, it is proper etiquette to use utensils such as a fork or spoon to eat your food. Picking food with your fingers can be messy and unclean, and it can also create the perception of a lack of manners.

Using utensils, such as a fork, knife, or spoon, to handle food is seen as a sign of good manners and shows respect for oneself and the company one is dining with. Utensils also help to prevent the spread of germs.

In some cultures, the type of utensils and cutlery and the way they are held or used can vary, but the general rule is to use them rather than one's hands. In some formal dining situations, specific utensils may be assigned for specific foods, and it is important to use the correct utensil to show proper etiquette.

When eating finger foods such as sandwiches, chicken wings, or French fries, it is okay to eat them with your hands, but it is still considered polite to use a napkin to wipe your hands before and after eating.

2.5 Do Not Play with Food

Teaching children not to play with their food while eating is important. Playing with food can be messy, unhygienic, and disrespectful to the person who prepared the meal. Additionally, it can also be a sign of a lack of manners.

Playing with food can also be a sign of disinterest or lack of appetite, and it can also be a way to waste food. Playing with food can include behaviors such as pushing food around on the plate, stacking or arranging food in an unnatural way, or using utensils to make designs or shapes with the food.

In formal dining situations, playing with food can particularly be disruptive and detract from the overall ambiance of the dining experience. In more casual settings, playing with food may still be considered inappropriate and impolite, especially if it is done in a way that is wasteful or offensive to others.

2.6 Do Not Talk with Food in the Mouth

It is considered impolite to talk with food in your mouth while eating. This can be unhygienic, as bits of food can be sprayed or expelled from the mouth, and it can also be difficult for others to understand what you're saying. You must wait until you have finished chewing and swallowing your food before speaking.

When speaking with food in the mouth, it can be difficult to understand what is being said, and it can also be unsightly. The food in the mouth can also create a potential health hazard, as it can be accidentally inhaled or spewed, spreading germs and making a mess.

2.7 Chew Silently

It is considered politer to chew with your mouth closed as well, as it can be visually unappealing to see someone chewing with their mouth open.

It is also important to remind children that they should be mindful of the sounds they make while eating and to be aware of the people around them.

Encouraging children to eat slowly and chew their food well can also help them enjoy their food more and be mindful of what they eat.

2.8 Converse with Everyone at The Table

An excellent method to develop a sense of community and create a welcoming environment is to engage in conversation with everyone at the table while eating. Sharing news and anecdotes with loved ones and friends while enjoying a meal together can be a fantastic way to catch up.

It is also considered a good manner to engage in conversation with everyone during the meal, not just focusing on one person or talking to only a selected few.

2.9 Ask for The Food to Be Passed

Children learn by example, so be sure to use polite language and manners when asking for food to be passed. Have your child practice asking for food to be passed during family or pretend meals.

Could you keep it simple? "Can you please pass the bread?" or "Could I have some more vegetables?" Gently remind them to ask for food to be passed if they forget.

2.10 Keep the Elbows and Other Body Parts Off the Table

Show them the correct posture and positioning for sitting at the table. If they forget, remind them to sit where their arms and body must be, away from the table. Praise and encourage them when they remember to keep their elbows and other body parts off the table.

Create a little game or challenge to see who can sit with the best posture and manners.

Color It

CHAPTER 3: LEARN MANNERS THROUGH FUN ACTIVITIES

It can be simpler and less terrifying than you think to teach children about table setting and encouraging good manners. We have put together some helpful advice to assist you get started on the path to bringing a little order and tranquility to the table.

Here are some creative suggestions for teaching your kids proper table etiquette.

3.1 All Set Out

Young toddlers might need to memorize the cutlery's placement and location. With this entertaining placemat, matching the photos makes it simple to know where to put everything!

Here is a fun activity to teach kids table-setting skills:

Table Setting Activity

Prepare a table with a tablecloth and place settings for each child. Give each child a set of utensils, plates, and glasses, and have them practice setting the table.

Have them identify each item and its proper placement, including the fork, knife, spoon, plate, glass, and napkin. Once they have learned table setting, have a mock meal and make them use the utensils and place settings correctly.

After the meal, have them clear the table and reset it correctly. Repeat the process a few

times to reinforce their understanding of table setting. You can also have a quiz session or a reward system for the kids who do well to make the activity more fun and engaging. Make use of paper placemat to learn how to set the table. Children must learn where the cutlery belongs each night. With this entertaining placemat, matching the photos makes it simple to know where to put everything!

3.2 Demonstrate a Game Play

Start by preparing a table with a tablecloth and place settings for each child. Make sure each place setting has a plate, knife, fork, spoon, glass, and napkin. Have the kids take turns to set the table. Give them verbal instructions, such as "Please place the fork on the left side of the plate," and have them repeat the instruction back to you to ensure they understand.

Once the table is set, you can cover it with a tea towel and remove one item. Ask the kids to identify what item is missing and where it belongs to. Repeat this process several times, gradually increasing the complexity of the task by removing more items or covering up more of the table.

As the kids improve, you can add a timer to make the game more challenging and competitive. You can also add a point system, where the child with the most points at the end wins a prize. Points can be awarded for correctly setting, identifying missing items, or completing the task in a set amount of time. The game is a great way to teach kids table-setting skills while improving their memory and focus. And, because it's a game, the kids will be more likely to enjoy it and learn the skills faster and more easily.

3.3 Stylish Napkins

By asking the youngsters to make different things with the napkins, you may turn the family dinner into a time for learning through enjoyable activities. Get a pack of paper napkins from the store to start. Any color or pattern that the youngsters like can be chosen. Each youngster should have a napkin in front of them on the table. Show the children various napkin folds, including the standard triangle, the fan, the flower, and the swan.

Give the kids a few minutes to practice folding their napkins. Please encourage them to get creative and try new designs. Once they have mastered the basics, you can have a napkin folding competition, where each child tries to create the most impressive design.

To make the activity more engaging, you can assign a theme to each dinner, such as a holiday or a special occasion, and have the kids create napkin designs that fit the theme. Not only will this activity spruce up family dinner time, but it will also help the kids develop their fine motor skills and creativity. Since it's a fun and interactive activity, the kids will be more likely to remember what they've learned.

34 Establish Place Setting

Use construction paper and markers to create place cards. Have each child make a place card for each family member and write their name. Then, they can place the cards at each setting.

Create custom plates and utensils using air-dry clay. The kids can make a plate and utensils for each family member and then use them for dinner. Decorate plain white plates with paint or markers. Have the kids draw designs, write names, or paint pictures on each plate.

Use fabric scraps to make napkins and table runners. Have the kids sew or tie the scraps together to create fun and unique place settings. Create unique glassware by decorating glasses with stickers, paint, or markers. Have the kids make a glass for each family member to use during dinner. Use paper or cardboard to make a table centerpiece. Have the kids make a fun and colorful decoration in the center of the table.

Turn the activity into a game by timing each child to see how quickly they can set the table. It can be a fun way to encourage competition and improve their speed. Turn the activity into a craft session by incorporating different materials, such as beads, ribbon, and glitter, to decorate the place settings.

3.5 The Scavenger Hunt for Silverware

The Scavenger Hunt for Silverware "is an entertaining and engaging exercise for kids. This activity aims to locate and arrange various utensils on a table in their proper locations. To play this game, serving plates, forks, knives, and spoons are hidden throughout the space. The children are then given a list of items to find. Their search for all the pieces is timed. The winner is the first to locate every piece of equipment and arrange it properly on the table. This activity teaches the youngsters how to correctly set the table while simultaneously entertaining them and helping them develop their hand-eye coordination and dexterity.

3.6 The Test of Setting the Table

"The Table Setting Challenge" teaches children how to prepare a table for a formal meal or special occasion. Each child needs to have a place setting consisting of a plate, cutlery, glass, and napkin. The kids' next task is preparing the table according to accepted etiquette guidelines. The children should arrange silverware appropriately, place the napkin on the left of the plate, and place the glassware and the plate should be positioned at the proper angles.

It enhances the children's skills and attention to detail and helps them develop important social skills and manners. As the kids can be timed and compared to one another to determine who can set the table the fastest and most precisely, it can also be a fun and competitive exercise.

3.7 The Manners Comparison

"The Manners Comparison" is a game that teaches children appropriate table manners and etiquette in a fun and instructive way. Finding the appropriate utensils to use with

various foods is the goal of this practice. Cut out photographs of various items, such as steak, spaghetti, soup, and salad, then arrange them on one side of the table to play this game. Place images of the necessary utensils on the other side, such as a knife and fork, soup spoon, and salad fork.

The kids then compete to match the food to the proper fork or spoon. This game teaches children to practice good table manners and highlights the significance of using the appropriate utensil for each type of food. Learning about various foods and utensils may also be entertaining and participatory. In addition, because the kids must think and match the appropriate pictures, it can enhance their cognitive abilities.

3.8 The Clothes Line

"The Clothes Line" is a simple and entertaining activity for youngsters that they can do during a party or mealtime. Folding napkins into various forms, such as a ball or a plane, and then taking turns throwing them against a set target, such as a plate or a glass. The objective is to see who can successfully direct the most napkins toward the target. This activity is adaptable to many skill levels and age groups, making it a flexible option for a variety of situations. Gather some folded napkins and a few targets, then invite the youngsters to take turns throwing the targets with their folded napkins. This game offers a great method to immerse kids in a creative and participatory game.

3.9 Drinking No-Spill Soup

Follow these steps to play "The No-Spill Soup Sip" table manners game:

To begin, demonstrate how to hold a spoon such that the bowl faces up and the handle is snugly positioned in the palm.

Give a bowl of soup and a spoon to each youngster.

Tell the kids to practice slurping soup slowly and deliberately while leaning the spoon to

one side. Please encourage them to savor their soup rather than eat it quickly.

Remind the children to use the No-Spill Soup Sip technique throughout the meal, taking care not to spill or splash soup.

Throughout the meal, give the kids encouraging feedback and praise for their good table manners and use of the No-Spill Soup Sip technique at home and in other mealtime settings.

3.10 The Calm Chew

The "Quiet Chew" activity is a fun way to teach children good table manners and encourage quiet and mindful eating. To play, have the kids sit at a table and start eating a snack or meal. The challenge is for them to chew their food as quietly as possible, and the first one to make a loud chewing noise loses. This activity helps to promote mindful eating and helps kids to develop good table manners, such as chewing with their mouths closed and not talking while they eat. It can also be a fun and interactive way to engage kids in a game that teaches them important life skills. You can give the winner a tiny prize or incentive, such as a piece of candy or a special treat, to heighten the excitement of the game. The "Quiet Chew" game is a fun approach to teach kids critical social skills they can use for the rest of their lives.

3.11 The Blindfolded Dining Challenge

The "Blindfolded Dining Challenge" is a fun and interactive activity that teaches kids about table manners and etiquette. The game's goal is for participants to eat a meal while blindfolded, using their sense of touch and taste to guide them.

To play, each participant is blindfolded and given a plate of food. They must then use their utensils to eat the meal without being able to see it.

This activity teaches kids about table manners and etiquette and helps develop their

sense of touch, taste, and smell. Additionally, the "Blindfolded Dining Challenge" promotes teamwork and communication as participants work together to identify the different foods they are eating.

You should supervise the game, and proper safety precautions should be taken, especially if young children are participating. Additionally, you should carefully select the food to ensure that it is safe for the participants to eat while blindfolded.

"The Polite Conversation Practice": Have the kids take turns having a conversation while eating, practicing good table manners and polite conversation skills.

3.12 The Utensil Relay Race

The "Utensil Relay Race" is a fun and interactive activity that teaches kids about proper table manners and etiquette. The game's goal is for teams to race against each other to see who can properly use their utensils to eat a meal the fastest.

To play, divide the participants into teams and give each team a set of utensils, such as forks, knives, and spoons. Each team member must then use the utensils to eat a designated food item, such as a piece of fruit or a sandwich, and then pass the utensils to the next team member. The first team to finish eating their meal using the proper table manners and etiquette wins the race.

This activity teaches kids about table manners and etiquette and promotes teamwork, communication, and physical coordination. The "Utensil Relay Race" can be easily adapted to different age groups and skill levels, making it a versatile choice for various occasions.

3.13 The Serving Etiquette Game

The game's goal is for participants to practice serving food to each other using proper table manners and etiquette.

To play, divide the participants into pairs or small groups and provide each group with a set of serving utensils and a platter of food. Each participant must then take turns serving the food to their partner or group members, using proper serving etiquette. It includes using utensils correctly, serving from the right side of the plate, and avoiding double-dipping or touching the food with their hands.

This activity teaches kids about serving etiquette and promotes teamwork, communication, and social skills. Additionally, the "Serving Etiquette Game" can be easily adapted to different age groups and skill levels, making it a versatile choice for various occasions.

3.14 The Table Manners Charades

"The Table Manners Charades" is a game that involves acting out different table manners and having other players guess what the action represents. The game is a fun approach to enforcing proper table manners while promoting social contact and communication.

To play "The Table Manners Charades," follow these steps:

Write down a list of different table manners on slips of paper, such as "chew with your mouth closed," "use a napkin," "sit up straight," "use utensils properly," and so on.

Have each player take turns drawing a slip of paper and silently acting out the table manner for the other players to guess.

Set a time limit for each round, such as 30 seconds, and have the other players guess the table manner before time runs out.

If the other players guess the table manner correctly, the acting player gets the point. If the other players cannot guess the table manner, no points are awarded. Play multiple rounds, each player taking turns acting out different table manners.

After the game, the player with the most points wins.

3.15 The Food Tasting Challenge

The "Food Tasting Challenge" is a fun and interactive activity that teaches kids about trying new foods and developing their sense of taste. The game's goal is for participants to taste various foods and guess what they are.

To play, set up a table with various foods, such as fruits, vegetables, cheeses, crackers, and dips. Each participant takes turns tasting a food, guessing what it is, and then moving on to the next food. The participant with the correct guesses at the end of the game wins.

3.16 The Table Setting Treasure Hunt

"Table Setting Treasure Hunt" is a fun and interactive activity that teaches kids about table setting and etiquette. The game's goal is for participants to search for and identify the correct placement of table-setting items, such as plates, silverware, glasses, and napkins.

To play, set the table with all of the necessary table-setting items and then hide one or more items in a designated area. Participants then take turns searching for the hidden items and placing them correctly on the table. The first participant to correctly place all of the hidden items wins.

3.17 The Manners Maze

To play "The Manners Maze," follow these steps:

Draw a maze on a large piece of paper or poster board. The maze should be complex enough to be challenging but not so difficult that it can't be completed within a few minutes.

Provide each child with a game piece, such as a small toy or game token.

Have the children take turns rolling a die or spinning a spinner to determine how many spaces they can move through the maze.

As each child navigates the maze, they must also follow the table manner indicated in each section of the maze. For example, if a child lands on a section of the maze that represents using a napkin, they must stop and demonstrate the proper way to use a napkin before continuing.

The first player to successfully navigate the maze while following the table manners wins the game.

3.18 The Food Group Bingo

The Food Group Bingo" is a fun and interactive activity that teaches kids about the different food groups and the importance of a balanced diet. The game's goal is for participants to match food items with the correct food group, such as fruits, vegetables, proteins, grains, and dairy.

To play, each participant is given a bingo card with different food group categories and food items listed. A caller then randomly calls out food items, and participants mark the items on their bingo cards if they have them. The first participant to match a horizontal, vertical, or diagonal row of food items with their corresponding food groups wins the game.

This activity teaches kids about the different food groups and the importance of a balanced diet and promotes healthy eating habits.

3.19 The Table Manners Trivia

Follow these steps to play "The Table Manners Trivia":

Make a list of trivia questions about good manners, such as "How should you handle your fork?" or "How do you decline a food you don't like politely?"

Put the kids into teams or let them play alone.

One trivia question per team or player should be asked at a time.

One point is awarded if the team or player who correctly responds to the question.

The opponent team or player can win the point by correctly answering the question if the team or person answers the question incorrectly.

After the game, the team or player with the most points wins.

3.20 The Pass the Pepper Game

The "Pass the Pepper Game" is a fun and interactive activity that teaches kids about proper table manners and etiquette. The game's goal is for participants to pass a pepper shaker from person to person around a table, following proper table manners and etiquette.

To play, participants sit around a table, and one participant starts by passing the pepper shaker to the person on their left. Each participant must then pass the pepper shaker to the next person, following proper table manners, such as using their right hand, passing the shaker with two hands, and avoiding touching the shaker with their elbows.

If a participant breaks any rule, they must start over, passing the pepper shaker back to the person they received it from. The goal is to pass the pepper shaker around the table, following proper manners and etiquette.

3.21 The Table Manners Talent Show

The "Table Manners Talent Show" is a creative and interactive activity that combines learning about proper table manners and etiquette with a performance aspect. The game's goal is for participants to showcase their table manners skills and creativity through performance.

To play, participants are divided into teams or compete individually. They then take turns performing various table manners tasks, such as properly using utensils, passing dishes and showing good posture. They can also perform creative skits or songs related to table manners.

Judges or the audience can score each performance based on their execution of proper table manners and their level of creativity. The team or individual with the highest score at the show's end wins.

3.22 The Food Art Contest

The "Food Art Contest" is a creative activity combining learning about healthy eating habits and artistic aspects. The game's goal is for participants to create beautiful and healthy works of food art using various fruits, vegetables, and other healthy ingredients.

To play, participants are given a set of ingredients, such as fruit, vegetables, nuts, and seeds, and asked to create a unique and visually appealing work of food art. They can use their creativity to create anything from fruit and vegetable animals to healthy landscapes.

Judges or the audience can score each creation based on their level of creativity, use of healthy ingredients, and overall presentation.

This activity teaches kids about healthy eating habits and the importance of incorporating fruits and vegetables into their diet and promotes creativity, problem-solving skills, and

imagination. Additionally, "The Food Art Contest" can be easily adapted to different age groups and skill levels, making it a versatile choice for various occasions.

3.23 Flash Card Activity

Write down different manners on separate index cards, such as "Say please," "Say thank you," "Wait for everyone to sit down before starting to eat," etc. Take a few minutes to review the flashcards with your children before mealtime. Discuss what each one means and how it should be used at the table

Place the flashcards in a pile on the table and have each child pick one before they start to eat. The child must follow the manners on their flash card during the meal. After each meal, mix up the flashcards and use a different set the next time.

You can make the flash card activity more fun by incorporating rewards, such as stickers or a prize for following all the manners during the meal. It will help to drive the message home and hopefully rub off on them just in time for dinner. Put it up on the wall.

CHAPTER 4: FUN ACTIVITIES TO TEACH GOOD BEHAVIOR AND TABLE MANNERS TO KIDS

Fun activities can be very important in teaching good behavior and table manners to kids because they make learning enjoyable and engaging. Children are more likely to be interested and motivated to learn when the activities are fun and interactive. Fun activities also provide a low-pressure environment where kids can make mistakes and learn from them without feeling discouraged.

4.1 Table Manners for Kids

Kids need to color the following picture of kids sitting on table.

Table Manners for Kids	
Name: _____	Date: _____

4.2 Good Table Manners Match-Up

Match-up both the columns with appropriate words to make a sentence.

Name: _____	Date: _____
Match the Columns	

Eat with		**a fork**
Please pass		**the food**
Chew with		**your mouth closed**
Wipe Your Mouth		**with a napkin**

4.3 Circle Good Table Manners

Ask kids to look at the worksheet carefully and circle the manners they think are good.

Circle Good Table Manners

Name: _____		Date: _____	
Wash hands	Eat over plate	Sit Nicely	Chew with mouth closed
Use spoons and knives			Use a Napkin
Wait for everyone to sit down	Slurping	Play with toys	Clear dishes

44 Table Manners Rules Poster

Ask your kids to read the table manners poster and try to remember the rules.

Table Manners Rules Poster

Name: _____ | Date: _____

Use your knife and fork whenever you eat something.

Don't throw food.

Eat with your mouth closed.

Don't speak with your mouth full.

Don't make a mess.

No tipping or spilling.

Don't use your fingers to eat.

Ask to be excused if you want to leave.

Don't kick under the table.

No toys at the table.

4.5 Write Good Manners You Have

Ask your kids to write what good manners they practice in front of others.

Write 7 Good Manners You Have

Name: _____

Date: _____

4.6 Using Table Manners

Place a chart having different good manners in a place where kid can have a look while moving around. You can take an example from the following worksheet.

Table Manners for Kids

	Napkin in your lap	
5		**Chew with Your Mouth Closed**
		Food to mouth, not mouth to food
	PLEASE AND THANK YOU	**Use your Please and Thank You**
	Take up your dishes when finished eating	

4.7 My Food Utensils

Help your kids to understand and solve the following practicing worksheet to Know about the utensils used in eating.

My Food Utensils	
Name: _____	Date: _____
Write missing alphabets to complete the words.	
_ _ r k	G l _ _ s
K n _ _ e	C _ _
S p _ _ _ _	P l _ _ e

CHAPTER 5: DINING ETIQUETTE & TABLE MANNERS

Because we know how to conduct ourselves at the dinner table and exhibit polite behavior, we are considered civilized beings. Not only is eating a need, but it is also a ritual that shares our well-being with others and demonstrates respect and decency for them.

With our family, friends, and business colleagues, eating out is a huge opportunity to demonstrate our intelligence and good manners.

We all observe other people's behavior and make evaluations of it, whether positive or negative. Our "breeding," not in a genetic sense, but rather in the way we have been educated, is reflected in our table manners. It is not a coincidence that every society on earth, whether ancient and modern, has a particular dining ritual. Breaking this table etiquette has always been considered unfavorable because the table is where our humanity is most clearly on display.

Some common elements of dining etiquette include:

Table manners: This includes using utensils properly, chewing with your mouth closed, not talking with food in your mouth, and avoiding behaviors like playing with food or reaching across the table.

Place setting: Knowing the proper placement of utensils, glasses, and plates can help guests feel more at ease during a meal.

Serving etiquette: Knowing how to serve and pass food, pour drinks, and handle serving dishes can help ensure a smooth and enjoyable dining experience.

Here are some points for teaching kids how to pass food, pour drinks, and handle serving utensils:

- The serving dish should be brought to the table and set on a trivet or hot pad.

- Food should be placed on individual plates using serving utensils.

- Hold the serving bowl with one hand while serving with the other.

- Pass the dish to the left to allow everyone to feed themselves.

- The beverage you want to pour should be filled in a pitcher or decanter.

- Stand up straight, and pour gently holding the pitcher or decanter in both hands.

- Pour the beverage in a glass leaving space for ice if preferred.

- Before sitting down, make sure everyone has a drink and offer to pour beverages for others.

- Hold the serving dish firmly in both hands when transporting it.

- When serving hot dishes, cover the table with a trivet or hot pad.

- Lifting a serving dish's lid can let hot steam out, so be cautious.

- Ask for assistance or use serving tongs if a dish is particularly heavy.

When serving and passing food, pouring beverages, and handling serving dishes, always be kind, patient, and practice good table manners.

Host and Guest Etiquette: In formal settings, it is important to know the proper roles and responsibilities of the host and guests during a meal.

Following are the proper roles and duties of the host and visitors during a lunch for children:

Host:

- Create a menu, then make the food.

- Plates, utensils, glasses, and napkins should be placed on the table.

- Welcome visitors upon arrival and check on everyone's comfort.

- Serve the meals and beverages.

- Make sure everyone is included in the conversation by taking the lead.

- Follow the meal with cleanup.

Guests:

- Be on time and appropriately dressed.

- Offer to assist the host with setup or cleanup.

- Use polite table manners, such as thank you and please, and refrain from talking while you are eating.

- Respect others and speak kindly to them.

- Talk in turn with others and pay close attention when they are speaking.

- Offer to help with the cleanup and thank the host for the meal.

- Kids can learn how to be excellent hosts and guests during mealtime by adhering to these roles and responsibilities. Everyone will have a nice and delightful dining experience if everyone is courteous, considerate, and respectful of one another.

Dress code: In formal dining situations, it is often expected that guests will dress appropriately, such as wearing formal attire or dressing smartly.

Dining etiquette can vary from culture to culture and even from one social setting to another. However, it is important to be aware of and follow the expected etiquette in each situation to show respect for others and to make mealtime a positive and enjoyable experience for all.

5.1 How Do You Start?

Start on the exterior and work your way in. When using a full set of silverware, feel comfortable by starting with the outermost utensils and working your way in during each meal.

In the US, the salad fork is usually the utensil that is placed on the utmost left and side.

You start from the outside and work your way inside because salad is typically one of the first courses. In several European traditions, salad is frequently served as the final course, hence the salad fork may occasionally be used.

Informal Table Setting

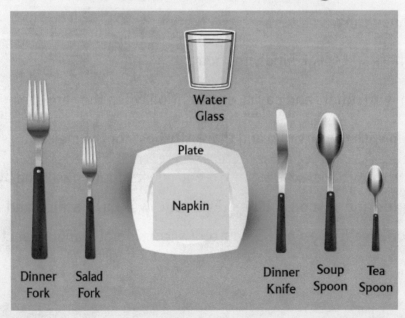

5.2 DRINK & BREAD

To help you remember where your drink and bread plate are, use this clever trick. Use the thumb and forefingers of your left hand to form the letter "b" for bread, and those of your right hand to form the letter "d" for a drink.

b	d

bread	**drink**

5.3 THE NAPKINS' RULES

The first thing you do when sitting at a table is place the napkin in your lap. You should wait to place your napkin on your lap until the host or hostess does so out of respect. We advise folding the napkin into a wide triangle or rectangle to give yourself numerous clean surfaces to deal with in case you spoil one side. Never roll up a napkin into a ball or use it as a bib. In a relaxed atmosphere, you can properly fold your napkin and place it to the left of your place setting when you leave the table. In a formal setting or restaurant, you may place your napkin on your seat. When you return to the table, it's crucial to remember not to sit on your napkin. Occasionally, in upmarket restaurants, the server will take your napkin while you are away from the table and then hand it back to you.

5 Napkin Rules	
	Place napkin according to the local table setting etiquette
	Fold in a simple way
	Place napkin on your lap
	Use it frequently but keep it clean
	Fold your napkin when leaving the table

5.4 Bread Breakage

Slice bread, muffins, or rolls into little pieces and eat one at a time. Put a modest quantity of butter on your bread plate by taking it from the communal bowls. The best course of action would be for you to stop sticking your bread knife into the shared butter bowl. Breaking bread has many historical and religious origins.

5.5 Salt and pepper

Salt and pepper should never be kept apart. Salt and pepper usually go together and are available in black and white, just like penguins. If someone only asks for one, always give them both. Make sure your fingertips are kept away from the tops of the salt and pepper shakers when holding them at the base. Place the salt and pepper on the table between you and the person to your right,

5.6 Rules for Soup Eating

Always ladle soup with a gentle scooping motion away from you. Before you can take up a bowl of soup and drink it, it must meet both of the following criteria:

1. The soup is served in a tiny cup without a thick lip around the outside.

2. After all the solids (vegetables, chicken, etc.) have been taken out, only the broth must be left.

When finished, place your soup spoon on the plate it was served on, as seen in the illustration to the left. Always keep your spoon away from the empty bowl.

Soup Eating Rules	
Sip, don't slurp.	
Always scoop from the side of the spoon.	
Avoid stirring the soup.	
Avoid blowing the soup.	
Add few crackers at one time.	
Don't dunk bread into the soup.	
You can tilt the bowl away from you to get the last drop.	

5.7 Dining Manners

How To Use a Breadknife?

Similar to how you would hold a surgical scalpel, hold the item.

Utensils should be placed in such a way that their tines point down. Your pointer finger should be resting against the back of your neck, the handle's end should be in contact with the center of your palm. You should pick the food with utensil and hold it securely.

Method Using a Pen

Like a pencil, hold the fork and spoon in your hands. It should lay between the tips of your middle and pointer fingers with your thumb on top to keep it secure. The webbing of your hand should be in close proximity to the utensils like fork and spoon.

Instead of switching hands while eating, place food on your fork with the help of your knife. Holding both utensils with the tines of the fork down, take a mouthful.

American Style

Use the other hand to pick up your fork while cutting your food and setting your knife down with the blade facing you. Consume while holding the tines upright.

kindly proceed with the right-hand side.

Pass serving trays, salt, pepper, and condiments on right side. There will only be an exception if the requester is to your immediate left.

American Style Table Setting

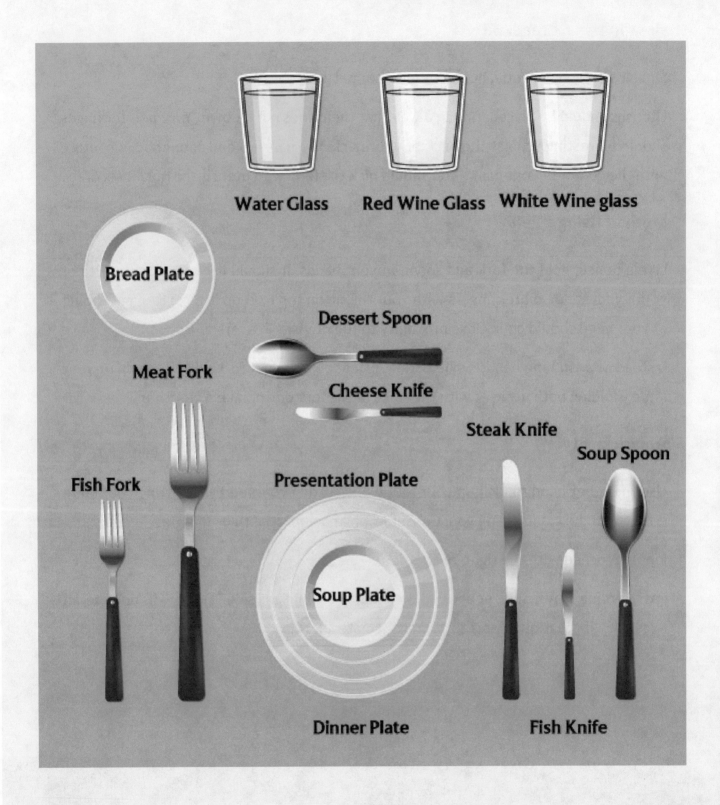

Water Glass   Red Wine Glass   White Wine glass

Bread Plate

Dessert Spoon

Meat Fork

Cheese Knife

Steak Knife

Soup Spoon

Fish Fork

Presentation Plate

Soup Plate

Dinner Plate   Fish Knife

Style: European/Continental Style Cutlery Holding

Utensils should be perpendicular to one another while dining continentally, with each handle on opposing sides of the plate and the knife's blade facing you to let your waiter know you have not completed. Make sure the fork tines are pointing DOWN toward the plate when using the continental style.

Different Styles of Holding Cutlery

5.8 My Healthy Plate

"My Healthy Plate" is a visual tool that can be used to teach kids about balanced and nutritious meal planning. The plate is divided into four sections: fruits, vegetables, protein, and grains. The idea is to fill each section of the plate with a specific type of food to ensure that the meal is balanced and nutritious.

My Healthy Plate	
Name: _____	Date: _____
Cut out the pictures below and paste them on your plate to create a healthy and complete meal.	

Fruits

Protein

Grain

Vegetable

Dairy

5.9 Table Rules

Teaching table rules to children is essential and it can help them understand expectations and boundaries, develop self-discipline and self-control, and learn how to behave on table and before others. Furthermore, table rules and eating behaviors provide a framework for children to learn and practice what they learn. Overall, teaching table manners and eating behaviors help children develop good eating habits that will benefit them throughout their lives.

Dinner Table Checklist	
Name: _____	**Date:** _____
Write Yes in the boxes of check list that you do	
Wash your hands before meal.	
Place your napkin on the lap.	
Chew with your mouth closed.	
Don't talk with your mouth full.	
Don't slurp.	
Wipe your mouth with your napkin.	
Lean over your plate.	
Use the right utensils.	
Learn to set the table appropriately.	
Say Please and Thank You.	

5.10 Setting the Table

Teaching children how to set a table is an important life skill that can help them develop social and cognitive abilities. Setting a table properly requires children to pay attention to details, follow instructions and practice fine motor skills. It also helps them to learn about etiquette and manners, which are important for social interactions.

Table Setting Vocabulary

Name: _____	Date: _____

Find and circle the vocabulary words in the grid. Look for them in all directions including backwards and diagonally.

```
R G E X Z A I K E N I G A T W R D Q D
T E P A N B Y R S H B T G G E U G Z B
P H K I Q V U O U F G S L V U A B W R
G T H A I C C F T S H T L Q H A X Q K
U O M I H A L E U S A A R E G R A H C
M L K G D S X I T A S U O S H X S K K
T C R W L S T V J L N B C Y A A N E E
B E J A R E F L H G D T T E M T R A Y
K L I X U R S J A Q B D P O B Q I R L
C B Z X N O P J U S F O V N T O E V S
H A K T N L O Z Q G C A W Z O T A S V
R T A M E E O K V M R I R L T R S T T
T K C M R Y N I N Z P K C A S O A C O
C T Z P U M E I R J J B L O T F U K P
F N H G J F K V T O N P C F Q A C A A
S E C E I P R E T N E C N J C B E O E
F C L N A F X L F A N I K E M A R Y T
U U K N X P I T C H E R T U R E E N E
U P L A T E Y S L D U W R G J T H A D
```

Bowl
Casserole
Centerpiece
Charger
Cup
Fork
Glass
Jug
Knife
Mug
Napkin
Pitcher
Plate
Platter
Ramekin
Runner
Salt Shaker
Solver
Samovar
Sauce Boat
Saucer
Spoon
Tablecloth
Taine
Teapot
Tray
Tureen

5.11 Good Table Manners Crossword

Help your kids to solve following table manners crossword.

Label the Table Setting

Name: _____	Date: _____

Word Bank

Hands	Fork
Excuse Me	Closed
Knife	Reaching
Talk	Inside Voice
Please	Spoon
Table	Thank You

Across

4. Which utensil do you use while eating soup?

6. How do you chew with your mouth at the table?

7. What utensil do you use when you eat salad?

9. What should you never do when you have food in your mouth?

10. No _____ across the table

12. No elbows on the_____

Down

1. What do you say to someone when they do something for you?

2. What kind of voice do you use when you are at the dinner table?

3. What do you need to wash before you eat?

5. What polite word do you say when you ask for something?

8. What utensil do you use to cut food?

11. What do you say when you need to leave the table?

5.12 Label the Table Setting

By labeling the different items on a table setting, children learn about the proper way to use each item and how to behave at the table. The worksheet can introduce children to new words and terms related to table setting and etiquette.

Label the Table Setting

Name: _____	Date: _____

Write the names of the utensils.

5.13 Different Ways of Setting a Table

Following are different ways of setting table for different occasions.

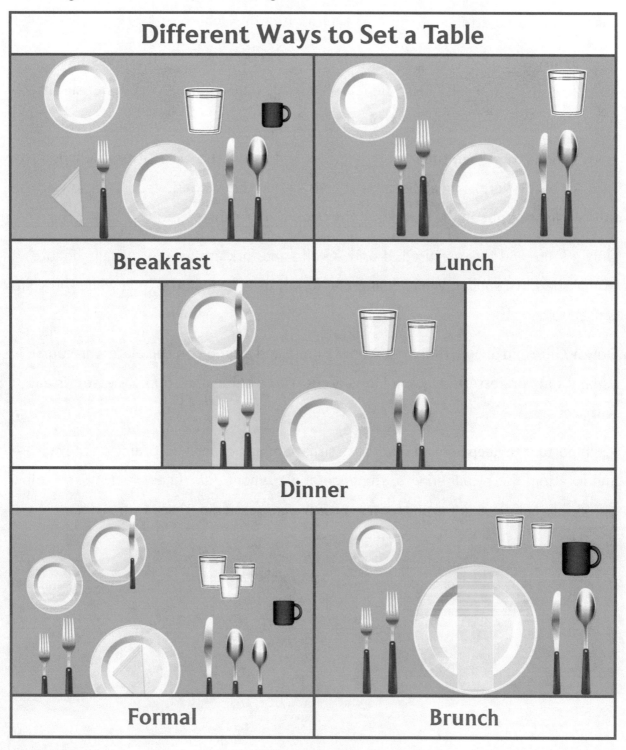

Different Ways to Set a Table

Breakfast · Lunch · Dinner · Formal · Brunch

5.14 Dinning Cutlery Rules

The arrangement of cutlery on a plate during a formal meal can reveal particular dining customs and etiquette. Here are some typical situations where cutlery is used:

Outside In: When the forks are put on the left side of the plate and the knives and spoons are placed on the right, it usually denotes a formal, multi-course meal. Start usig cutlery from the utnesils placed closest to your plate.

Above the Plate: When the cutlery is positioned above the plate, it typically denotes a buffet or less formal meal. Because the visitors in this scenario feed themselves, the utensils are not put on the plate until the people are ready to eat.

Only a knife and fork are used: If only a knife and fork are used, it usually denotes a formal sit-down supper. While dining, the fork is used to hold the food while the knife is used to chop it.

Only a Knife and Spoon: If there are only a knife and a spoon on the plate, the course is usually soup or dessert. Any solid food is cut with a knife, and soup or dessert is eaten with a spoon.

It's important to keep in mind that these situations can change according on the culture and location. But by adhering to the general placement guidelines, guests can exhibit ppropriate eating manners and leave a positive impression during a formal dinner.

Dining Cutlery Placement

Formal Multi-Course Table Setting	Buffet or Less Formal Table Setting

Formal Sit-down Supper	Soup or Dessert Table Setting

5.15 What Do Your Spoon and Fork Say?

Here are some ways to convey various messages throughout a meal while using a fork and spoon:

What do Your Fork and Knife Say?	
Start	Excellent
Do not Like	Finished
Pause	Ready for Second Plate

CONCLUSION

"Table Manners Workbook for Kids 4-12" is a valuable resource for parents and caregivers who want to teach their children good manners and etiquette. The workbook is filled with fun and interactive activities that make learning about table manners enjoyable for children. The activities cover a wide range of topics, from asking for food to be passed to keeping elbows and other body parts off the table to making eye contact and asking questions. Parents and caregivers can use the workbook to teach children how to behave appropriately in different settings, such as at home, school, or public. By consistently practicing the activities in this workbook, children will learn important social skills that will serve them well throughout their lives.

THANK YOU

Made in the USA
Thornton, CO
09/08/23 16:47:37

05c5c77a-be0b-4697-bea5-a41823a917d7R01